THE PASSION OF CHRIST

I0171352

Study by Layne Smith
Commentary by Cecil Sherman

Free downloadable Teaching Guide for this study available at

NextSunday.com/teachingguides

NextSunday Resources
6316 Peake Road
Macon, Georgia 31210-3960
1-800-747-3016
©2014 by NextSunday Resources
All rights reserved.

TABLE OF CONTENTS

The Passion of Christ

HOW TO USE THIS STUDY

NextSunday Resources Adult Bible Studies are designed to help adults study Scripture seriously within the context of the larger Christian tradition and, through that process, find their faith renewed, challenged, and strengthened. We study the Scriptures because we believe they affect our current lives in important ways. Each study contains the following three components:

Study Guide

Each study guide lesson is arranged in four movements:

Remembering provides a frame of reference for the Scriptures.

Studying is centered on giving the biblical material in-depth attention while often surrounding it with helpful insights from theology, ethics, church history, and other areas.

Understanding helps us find relevant connections between our lives and the biblical message.

What About Me? provides brief statements that help unite life issues with the meaning of the biblical text.

Commentary

Each study guide lesson is accompanied by an additional, in-depth commentary on the biblical material. Written by a different author than the study guide, each commentary gives the opportunity for learners to approach the Scripture text from a separate but complementary viewpoint.

Teaching Guide

In addition to the provided study guide and commentary, *NextSunday Resources* also provides a *free* downloadable teaching guide, available at NextSunday.com. Each teaching guide gives the teacher tools for focusing on the content of each study guide lesson through additional commentary and Bible background information. Through teacher helps and teaching options, each teaching guide also provides substance for variety and choice in the preparation of each lesson.

NextSunday
Resources

STUDY INTRODUCTION

We see in the Passion of Christ our own struggle of faith. Authentic faith is a daily challenge. According to Hebrews 11:1, "faith is the assurance of things hoped for, the conviction of things not seen." On our good days, we may reflect this kind of faith. The problem is, we have bad days. Life and the life of faith are not always easy. For this reason, we are encouraged to gather together for fellowship, study, and worship. We find strength and help for faithful living in the context of the church of Jesus Christ.

Sometimes, faith seems like a "two steps forward and one step back" proposition. As Frederick Buechner reminds us: "Faith is better understood as a verb than as a noun, a process than as a possession. It is on-again-off-again rather than once-and-for-all. Faith is not being sure where you're going but going anyway. A journey without maps" (Buechner, 25).

We need not feel guilty that faith is not always easy for us. Have you ever been traveling in unfamiliar territory? There is no shame in having a difficult time finding your way. Stopping to ask for directions is part of the journey. Heading down the wrong road from time to time is all but inevitable. The question is not whether we will go down the wrong roads in our faith journey. All of us will. The question is whether we will find the resources to acknowledge our failure, turn from it, and learn from it.

The four lessons in this unit highlight the faith struggles of the early disciples. In lesson one, Jesus addresses the issues of faith and practice. In lesson two, we meet Judas, who like us, struggled with God's Kingdom and human kingdoms. In lesson three, the issue of temptation reminds us that our faith journey is a constant challenge. Lesson Four invites us to remember Peter's experience of "faith failure." Peter's failure, however, is not the final word. There is forgiveness.

Frederick Buechner, Wishful Thinking: A Theological ABC (New York: Harper & Row, 1973).

1

PRACTICING OUR FAITH

Matthew 23:1-3, 29-39

Central Question

Why is it important for practice to be consistent with faith?

Scripture

Matthew 23:1-3 Then Jesus said to the crowds and to his disciples, 2 "The scribes and the Pharisees sit on Moses' seat; 3 therefore, do whatever they teach you and follow it; but do not do as they do, for they do not practice what they teach."

Matthew 23:29-39 "Woe to you, scribes and Pharisees, hypocrites! For you build the tombs of the prophets and decorate the graves of the righteous, 30 and you say, 'If we had lived in the days of our ancestors, we would not have taken part with them in shedding the blood of the prophets.' 31 Thus you testify against yourselves that you are descendants of those who murdered the prophets. 32 Fill up, then, the measure of your ancestors. 33 You snakes, you brood of vipers! How can you escape being sentenced to hell? 34 Therefore I send you prophets, sages, and scribes, some of whom you will kill and crucify, and some you will flog in your synagogues and pursue from town to town, 35 so that upon you may come all the righteous blood shed on earth, from the blood of righteous Abel to the blood of Zechariah son of Barachiah, whom you murdered between the sanctuary and the altar. 36 Truly I tell you, all this will come upon this generation. 37 "Jerusalem, Jerusalem, the city that kills the prophets and stones those who are sent to it! How often have I desired to gather your children together as a hen gathers her brood under her wings, and you were not willing! 38 See, your house is left to you, desolate. 39 For I tell you, you will not see me again until you say, 'Blessed is the one who comes in the name of the Lord.'"

Remembering

This lesson begins a study of Matthew's account of Christian *Holy Week*. For Jesus and his followers, it was *Passover Week*.

Jerusalem was full of faithful Jews who had gathered to remember, rehearse, and relive the story of God's deliverance of the Jews from the Egyptian pharaoh through Moses' leadership. This story was THE formative event in the life of the Jews. Celebrating it annually helped them to remember their history. God's mighty acts on their behalf set them free from captivity in Egypt.

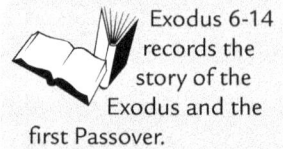

Exodus 6-14 records the story of the Exodus and the first Passover.

Remembering the past provided them hope for their future. God, who had cared for them faithfully in their past, surely would do the same in the days, years, and generations to come. This week, for Jesus' followers, will be a week of remembering God's deliverance in the past, but also will serve to provide deliverance, through the death, burial, and resurrection of Jesus, for all eternity. Deliverance or salvation will become a very present reality, neither something simply remembered in the past nor something merely hoped for in the future.

In today's text, Jesus has already entered Jerusalem, beginning the final week of his life before the Crucifixion. This passage in Matthew, beginning with 23:1, is the final section of teaching in this Gospel.

Studying

The first of the week (23:1-2) On Tuesday, Jesus addresses the crowds and his disciples. The crowds represent potential disciples of Jesus. Specifically, though, this message is directed toward the church and its leaders (Craddock, 260).

The scribes were formally trained, professional Jewish leaders. Similar to present-day lawyers, they were trained in understanding and interpreting Jewish law. The Pharisees, on the other hand, were mostly laypersons without any formal theological education, who attempted to follow the strict religious rules outlined by the scribes. Although some scribes were Pharisees, few Pharisees were scribes. "'Moses seat' is a symbolic expression representing the teaching and administrative authority of the synagogue leadership, scribes and Pharisees" (Boring, 430-31).

Actions speak louder than words (23:3) This verse contains no disrespect for Moses and the law (or Scripture). It does, however, warn against following the teachers' actions rather than their teaching. The teaching may be sound and true, although Jesus is by no means endorsing everything that they taught. Jesus does call into question some of their teachings in other passages. This text, though, focuses on the actions of these teachers and preachers that may lead one astray.

"Woe" is an interjection used to express sorrow, grief, regret, or distress or a noun signifying a condition of deep suffering due to a calamity. Although the interjection almost always clearly expresses a declaration of lament (see Num 21:29; 1 Sam 4:7-8; Ps 120:5; Eccles 4:10; Isa 24:16; Jer 10:19, 45:2; Lam 5:16; Mic 7:1; Mt 24:18; 1 Cor 9:16), in many cases it serves primarily as a curse or denunciation (see Isa 45:9-10; Jer 22:13, 23:1; Ezek 13:18, 16:23; Hos 7:13; Mt 18:7; Mk 14:21; Lk 6:20-26; Rev 12:12). The term is used frequently by the prophets in oracles of judgment against cities (e.g., Jer 13:27; Ezek 24:6, 9; Zeph 3:1; cf. Mt 11:21 par. Lk 10:13) (See Wyper, 1088).

"Like father, like son"; "Like mother, like daughter" (23:29-33)
Between our opening verse and these verses, Jesus offers six "woes." "Woes," used by the Old Testament prophets (Isa 45:9-10; Jer 13:27; 48:46; Ezek 16:23), is a literary form used by a speaker to address someone not actually present.

Verses 29-33 record Jesus' seventh "woe." Jesus calls the scribes and the Pharisees hypocrites. The primary meaning of "hypocrite" in this passage is not insincerity but inconsistency between one's beliefs and one's actions, regardless of whether one is aware of that inconsistency. This understanding of the word helps make the connection between Jesus' warning first seen in verse 3 (Boring 434-435).

By describing the Jewish method for honoring dead prophets—building tombs and decorating graves—Jesus is telling his listeners that they likely would have been among those who persecuted and killed prophets in the earlier days. Within the week, they will contribute to his death, the death of one who is far greater than any of the prophets (Robertson, 184). They will continue to persecute others that God sends to prophesy. The people's claim to honor the prophets of God while they are at the same time contributing to their demise is a case of saying one thing and then doing the opposite. There is no integrity to a life with so much difference between what one says and what one does. "When a prophet is dead, he can no longer disturb our selfish comfort. We can praise him then and make the praise a substitute for courageous righteousness in our time" (Buttrick, 538). It is easy and acceptable for us to identify with the prophets of yesteryear, for they are safely dead.

Jesus is saying that those who hear his words are like their ancestors. The children of those who killed the prophets in the past will kill the prophets of the present and the future—"Like father, like son"; "like mother, like daughter." In verse 32, Jesus tells the listeners to "fill up the measure of your ancestors." In other words, "Go ahead and complete what your parents started" (Stagg, 214).

God's judgment (23:33-36) Such actions, however, are not without dire consequences. God's judgment on those who say one thing and do another, all in the name of God, is just around the corner.

The Hebrew word translated as "hell" is *Gehenna*. It refers to the "Valley of Hinnom," a ravine located just south of Jerusalem. Because this valley had been the site of idol worship during Old Testament times (2 Kgs 23:10; 2 Chr 23:8; Jer 7:31), it had become a garbage dump where a fire burned continually. By the time of this Gospel's writing, the term *Gehenna* had come to represent the fiery judgment of God (Boring, 436).

Jesus' words are harsh. Perhaps they are the harshest of his words ever recorded. Jesus wants his hearers to have the opportunity to understand what is at stake. If they, like their ancestors, continue persecuting those who come from God, then they will suffer God's judgment.

Abel and Zechariah are both mentioned in these

> The development of the valley of Hinnom as a metaphorical designation in the New Testament of the (final) state of torment for the wicked can be traced only in the extracanonical literature. In the New Testament, the idea of Gehenna is simply stated as understood and accepted. With the exception of James 3:6, Gehenna occurs only in the recorded teachings of Jesus, where it is apparent that Jesus assumed his hearers would understand what was meant by Gehenna (Rowell, 319).

verses. The Hebrew Bible began with Genesis and concluded with 2 Chronicles. Abel was the first victim of persecution (Gen), and Zechariah was the last messenger of God to be martyred (2 Chr). Those who participate in the persecution or killing of God's prophets bear in some way responsibility for the deaths of all God's prophets.

These words are the last the crowd hears Jesus speak before he departs with his disciples (24:1). Jesus calls for a decision from the crowd. The next time "the crowd" is mentioned is at Jesus' arrest (26:55). By then, they have found their answer. They have made their decision to line up against this prophet of God, God's own son (Boring, 436).

Jesus' grace (23:37-39) Jesus takes no joy in his final words in the Temple. He is thoroughly heartbroken. In these concluding words in which he uses the beautiful image of a mother hen's quickly gathering her chicks around her when danger is near, Jesus speaks movingly of his pain and his care for those who persist in rejecting him despite all his efforts.

Jesus offers grace, another opportunity for his hearers. The time is very near, though, when one's choice will have to be made.

Understanding

How easy it is for us to "talk" a better game than we "play." It is much easier to speak of faithful living than it is to live faithfully.

Our text for today, though, does not permit us to separate our practice from our beliefs. What we say we believe and how we live need to be consistent and harmonious.

What we believe *is* important. Jesus never questions this point. Just as there is no substitute for sound, correct doctrine, there is also no substitute for authentic, conscientious practice of our faith in our lives. Our convictions and our actions are two sides of the same coin. Ultimately and according to God's plan, our actions must match our faith convictions.

James 2:14-17 speaks of the "bankruptcy" of faith without practice. James reminds us that it does no good to tell a brother or a sister to stay warm and eat plenty if we do not assist them in staying warm and having plenty. Confessing our faith and practicing our faith are not "either/or" issues for Christians. It is "both/and." The Scriptures are clear that God expects us to live with integrity. Synonyms for "integrity" include: "character," "honesty," "honor," and "principle." In other words, the Bible calls us to live whole, seamless lives that are all of one piece. This faith journey calls for continual vigilance and commitment. Jesus is clear that we will be accountable for the ways we practice our faith.

God's prophets are still in our midst, calling us to live integrated lives of sound doctrine and authentic practice. Like the original audience of this text, it is easy for us to honor deceased prophets while discounting the words of those who currently serve as vehicles of God's message for us today.

How do we recognize God's prophets today? It is not an easy task. Sometimes, we allow our prejudices and biases to get in the way of our recognizing and hearing God's prophets. At other times we are blinded by the claims of a false prophet. Jesus cautions that the actions of prophets will not match their words in every case. Like us, they are human and flawed. Still, some of them teach us to follow the ways of God. Following the teachings of prophets takes courage and perseverance, but Jesus promised never to leave us or forsake us (Heb 13:5).

What About Me?

• *Our actions should be consistent with our words.* As is common with Jesus, he points to real-life situations as contemporary parables for his listeners. The religious leadership of his day was falling into the trap of doing one thing but telling people to do another. Do I fall into the trap of saying "do as I say, not as I do" to my family, friends, co-workers, and others? Do I live my life like the scribes and Pharisees to which Jesus refers?

• *Our actions clearly communicate what we believe.* The word *hypocrite* in Jesus' day described the abilities of an actor, a person who pretends to be different than he or she is. In our context, the word actor has a good connotation. We often applaud the actors who entertain us. Pretense, however, is not appropriate in relationships. In relationships, especially in our relationships with God, our actions are very clearly connected to our sincere convictions. Do I live my life with integrity? Is my conduct consistent with my confession of faith? Do I help or hinder God's work in the world with my words and deeds?

• *The words of God's prophets should not be ignored.* Am I honest about my prejudices and biases, particularly when confronted with someone who clearly articulates my long-held, cherished values and then compares them to the call to justice, mercy, and faithful living in Scripture?

Resources

W. Wyper, "Woe," *The International Standard Bible Encyclopedia*, vol. 4, ed. Geoggrey W. Bromiley (William B. Eerdman's Publishing, 1998).

PRACTICING OUR FAITH

Matthew 23:1-3, 29-39

Introduction

The lessons in March lead toward Calvary and Easter. They are taken from Matthew, and collectively they are difficult themes. Hypocrisy, betrayal, and denial are themes associated with Christ's last week on earth.

Jesus taught about 27 AD. The Church interpreted Jesus' words after the fall of Jerusalem in 70 AD. Then they were written by Matthew. So much "water had gone under the bridge" in the years between Jesus' speaking and Matthew's writing until "interpretation" by the Early Church could not be avoided. This "interpretation" does not diminish the power of what Jesus said, but it does force us to think carefully. Matthew "interpreted" Jesus' words considering the rise of the Early Church, the hostility that developed between Jew and Christian, and the fall of Jerusalem (In 70 AD, the Romans thoroughly destroyed Jerusalem and the temple). The commentators I read struggle to separate the words of Jesus from the interpretations of Matthew.

The setting for this passage is the last week of Jesus' ministry. It was Passover Week. Collectively, the gospel description of Jesus is a mild-mannered, patient, and forgiving person. When such a person's language becomes violent, it is time to take notice. To feel the power and anger of Jesus, read chapter 23 in its entirety. It is strong medicine. There is a sense of finality about this denunciation of "the scribes and the Pharisees" (Mt 23:2a). For three long years, Jesus had put up with the pestering and posturing of these religious leaders. In today's text, he unloads. George Buttrick cautions: "We shall be wise to give this passage a positive turn. What grace does Christ covet in his followers? The opposite of the sins here condemned" (*The Interpreter's Bible*, Vol. 7, New York: Abingdon Press, 1951, 530). Jesus' condemnation of the "scribes and Pharisees" could be used as a springboard to whatever rouses our ire. That's why Buttrick's caution is so necessary. Jesus was in a better place to condemn than we are.

I. Integrity, 23:1-3, "They do not practice what they teach."

A "scribe" was a student of the Law of Moses. "Moses' seat" was "probably the name given to the chair in the synagogue where the authoritative teacher of the law sat" (Sherman Johnson, *The Interpreter's Bible*, Vol. 7, 528). Jesus aimed his remarks at those interpreting the Law of Moses to the people. Today these people would be called preachers, for preachers interpret the Scriptures. To "sit on Moses' seat" is much like "to stand in the pulpit" today.

Jesus was careful to distinguish between teaching and practice. William Barclay interprets "What He is saying is this, 'Insofar as these Scribes and Pharisees have taught you the great principles of the Law which Moses received from God, you must obey them'" (*The Gospel of Matthew*, Vol. 2, Philadelphia: Westminster Press, 1958, 314-315). It is sad but true that bad characters can speak truth. W. T. Connor, professor of theology at Southwestern Seminary, said, "The Lord can strike some mighty straight licks with a crooked stick." So, Jesus said, "do whatever they teach you and follow it" (Mt 23:3).

After conceding that these people could speak the truth, Jesus went on to cite his first complaint against them, "but do not do as they do, for they do not practice what they teach" (Mt 23:3b). Built into preaching and teaching is the assumption that the one preaching is practicing what he or she is preaching. I tell my students your character is the platform you stand on when you preach.

When I was ten years old, my grandfather took me with him to the cotton gin. It was a chilly November day. Other farmers and the cotton buyer were there. The buyer came to the bales that belonged to Jim Brannon (my grandfather). With a brace and bit, the cotton buyer bore a hole in one of the cotton bales. He turned the brace until the bit had gone deep into the cotton. I asked my grandfather what the cotton buyer was doing. My grandfather said, "Some people put trash or rocks inside the cotton. He is boring a hole to see if cotton is all the way through the bale."

Years later, I was searching for an illustration of God's expectations of us at the Last Day. I wondered if God will drill a hole deep into my character to see if the things I've said in the pulpit are consistent with what's deep in my character. Good religion works to make the inside and the outside of us the same. We finally become what we profess to be. We have integrity if we are the same all the way through. If we teach it, we have to live it.

II. Identity, 23:29-32, "You are descendants of those who murdered the prophets."

When Jesus lived, memorials to prophets dotted the landscape of Jerusalem. These memorials were honored. There was a memorial to Jeremiah, but history records that Jeremiah was imprisoned, and had his eyes gouged out among other abuses. A pattern had emerged: Prophets were abused and often killed. But, when the truth of the prophet's message became clear to a slow people, *then* the same prophet who was abused in life would be honored in death.

Remember, Jesus will die in three days. He has come to God's chosen people with a new word, a larger revelation. As God is a prophet and more, he, too, was being abused by God's chosen people. These people honored Jeremiah six hundred years after Jeremiah died, now the descendants of those who tormented Jeremiah would kill Jesus.

A new word from God is hard to accept. Religious people have an especially hard time with new truth. Most of us think God's truth is frozen, that the truth we have is all God is ever going to reveal. Yet God keeps on revealing more. Two hundred years ago, slaves were sold in my town and women were second-class citizens. Four hundred years ago, witchcraft was taken seriously and only a few believed common people had judgment enough to order government or Church. All that's changed and most rejoice in the revelations that have brought these changes. Here and there are deep holes of resistance to all these changes, and the resistance is most often sandbagged behind somebody who is thumping on a Bible. Jesus knew their kind well.

So, who are "the descendants of those who murdered the prophets"? (Mt 23:31). It is not the ones who honor safely dead prophets. It is the few who recognize prophets in the present. Do I safely honor the prophet hundreds of years after? Do I hear and respond to the prophet when he or she speaks? Jesus lamented religious blindness among the people of his day. Only in hindsight did they recognize God's presence among them. And Jesus? They couldn't identify him.

In our day, Martin Luther King, Jr. held high the banner of fairness. He challenged this country to rise to the nobility of her creeds. You know what happened to King. Each year, the city of Atlanta receives more than a million people at the memorial for Martin Luther King. Interesting, he is honored in death. But he was too shrill, too aggressive in life. *We* ignore our prophets in life. *We* honor them in death. Not much has changed.

III. Prophecy, 23:33-36, "I send you prophets, sages and scribes..."

These verses are part prediction and part experience. Jesus was telling what *would* happen; Matthew was telling what *had* happened. Jesus said some things would happen; Matthew lived through them. Not surprisingly, Matthew's text is a combination of the two.

(1) Jesus said, "I send you prophets, sages and scribes, some of whom you will kill and crucify, and some you will flog in your synagogues and pursue from town to town" (Mt 23:34).

It happened just as Jesus predicted. The "prophets, sages, and scribes" were Christian evangels and they were persecuted. Stephen's death is recorded in Acts 7:54-8:1. "That day a severe persecution began against the church in Jerusalem, and all except the apostles were scattered throughout the countryside of Judea and Samaria" (Acts 8:1b). Paul is introduced in Acts as a persecutor of the Church (Acts 9:1-2).

(2) The reaction to Christian evangels would be no different from the reaction to the prophets of centuries past. The prophets of God's new truth would be killed. "Upon you may come all the

righteous blood shed on earth, from the blood of righteous Abel to the blood of Zechariah...Whom you murdered between the sanctuary and the altar" (Mt 23:35). Jesus is charging that humanity has a record of killing God-sent people. Cain murdered Abel and Zechariah's death is described in 2 Chronicles 24:20-22. In the Hebrew Bible, 2 Chronicles was the last book. Jesus is saying from the first (Abel) until the last (Zechariah) your record has been constant. You have murdered the people God has sent you. Israel's rejection of God-sent people was neither novel nor occasional; it was pattern.

(3) Jesus predicted the violence to Christian evangels would be immediate. "Truly I tell you, all this will come upon this generation" (Mt 23:36). By the time Matthew wrote, prediction had become reporting. Matthew wrote after 70 AD. Most of the disciples had met a violent death in Christ's service. Jesus spoke a curse on prophet abusers. "You snakes, you brood of vipers! How can you escape being sentenced to hell?" (Mt 23:33). Zechariah killers, Stephen killers. Both were prophets sent from God. They should command respect, not abuse.

IV. Rejection, 23:37-39—"Jerusalem,...How often have I desired to gather your children...and you were not willing."

The synoptics (Matthew, Mark, Luke) are set mainly in Galilee. Our text says Jesus had often been to Jerusalem. He had tried to minister there, but they would have no part of him. Two observations:
• Our gospels only highlight Jesus' ministry. "Now Jesus did many other signs in the presence of his disciples, which are not written in this book" (Jn 20:30). And again, "there are also many other things that Jesus did" (Jn 21:25a). Jesus was in Jerusalem at other times, but we know nothing of them.
• Jerusalem was hard territory for Jesus. The country people of Galilee were more open to Jesus' message than the people of Jerusalem. Orthodoxy can be a wonderful thing. It can also be a barrier to recognizing God's own dear Son.

The power of this text is in the earnestness of Jesus' reaching out to Jerusalem. Jesus was an evangelist. The town he wanted to influence the most was the place where he was least effective. Our text repeats: "Jerusalem, Jerusalem..." It reminds me of David's lament about the death of his wayward, rebellious son. "O my son Absalom, my son, my son Absalom! Would I had died instead of you. O Absalom, my son, my son!" (2 Sam 18:33). The death of a son is a terrible thing. What are we to say of the death of a dream, a mission?

Jesus was rejected. "He came to what was his own, and his own people did not accept him" (Jn 1:11). And Jesus was crushed. Jesus loved those people beyond anything I can have or know. It would seem the power of that love would have compelled a response. But what was vibrant in Jesus wakened nothing in the people to whom that love was offered. We know rejection. A child walks away from parents who have tried to be loving, caring parents. That's rejection. A romance goes sour. One party gives love; the other is dead to the offer. That's rejection. Imagine Jesus as the carrier of "the love of God," and his special mission was first, "Go nowhere among the Gentiles,...but go rather to the lost sheep of the house of Israel"...and you will begin to feel what Jesus felt (Mt 10:5-6). Speaking literally, we have to say the Romans killed Jesus. Speaking from the heart, Jerusalem's rejection killed Jesus.

Awful things would come to Jerusalem. In 70 AD, their headstrong ways brought down the wrath of Rome. Rome brought no "occupation." This destruction was total. It didn't have to be that way. Rejection and desolation traveled together and still do.

Notes

Notes

SELLING OUT

Matthew 26:14-25; 27:3-10

Central Question

How are we tempted to betray our faith?

Scripture

Matthew 26:14-25 Then one of the twelve, who was called Judas Iscariot, went to the chief priests 15 and said, "What will you give me if I betray him to you?" They paid him thirty pieces of silver. 16 And from that moment he began to look for an opportunity to betray him. 17 On the first day of Unleavened Bread the disciples came to Jesus, saying, "Where do you want us to make the preparations for you to eat the Passover?" 18 He said, "Go into the city to a certain man, and say to him, 'The Teacher says, My time is near; I will keep the Passover at your house with my disciples.'" 19 So the disciples did as Jesus had directed them, and they prepared the Passover meal. 20 When it was evening, he took his place with the twelve; 21 and while they were eating, he said, "Truly I tell you, one of you will betray me." 22 And they became greatly distressed and began to say to him one after another, "Surely not I, Lord?" 23 He answered, "The one who has dipped his hand into the bowl with me will betray me. 24 The Son of Man goes as it is written of him, but woe to that one by whom the Son of Man is betrayed! It would have been better for that one not to have been born." 25 Judas, who betrayed him, said, "Surely not I, Rabbi?" He replied, "You have said so."

Matthew 27:3

When Judas, his betrayer, saw that Jesus was condemned, he repented and brought back the thirty pieces of silver to the chief priests and the elders.

Remembering

Our lesson today spans three days of Holy Week—Wednesday, Thursday, and Friday. At the end of Matthew 25, Jesus concludes his teaching ministry. He has done his best to teach his disciples the ways of God's Kingdom. He has tried to prepare them for the challenges, victories, and defeats that they will face when he is no longer physically with them. At times, the disciples have been able to receive and understand Jesus' teaching. At other times, though, they appear to have been "spiritually challenged."

In the first verses of Matthew 26, the chief priests and elders seek to find a way to arrest and kill Jesus. Due to their fear that the people might riot, they decide to delay their plan until after the Passover.

In the verses immediately preceding the text for our lesson (26:6-13), a woman had poured costly ointment on Jesus as a beautiful sign of her love and gratitude for him. In today's lesson, we see a sharp contrast to one who gives love so generously. The woman was a giver whereas Judas is a taker, even to the point of betrayal.

From chapter 26 to the end of Matthew, Jesus observes the Passover with his disciples, institutes the Lord's Supper, and is arrested, crucified, and raised on the third day after his crucifixion.

Studying

Planning a betrayal (26:14-16) In these verses, Judas clearly took the initiative. He sought out the chief priests in order to betray

Jesus. His question "What will you give me if I hand Jesus over to you?" suggests that Judas was willing to betray Jesus because of his greed.

Why did Judas betray Jesus? Some suggest that Judas had become disillusioned because Jesus had not demonstrated the nationalistic, militaristic leadership that some Jews expected of the Messiah. Judas, according to this scenario, may have perceived that he was doing everyone a favor by ridding the world of Jesus. Others surmise that Judas saw Jesus as a divine leader, maybe even the Messiah. Perhaps Judas did not want Jesus to die, but was instead attempting to force Jesus into action, to show that Jesus really was the Messiah the Jews had anticipated. Judas refused to accept Jesus as he was and tried to make Jesus into the person he wanted him to be (Barclay, 332-333). Regardless of his motives and intentions, Judas betrayed Jesus for thirty pieces of silver.

> Thirty pieces of silver can be traced back to Zechariah 11:12. The owner of an ox who gores a slave is commanded to pay the slave-owner thirty pieces of silver, a small amount (Ex 21:32) (Schweizer, 488).

Why was it necessary for Jesus to be "betrayed" or "delivered"? Jesus was a public person. His whereabouts were likely no big secret. The information Judas supplied the chief priests allowed them to apprehend Jesus in a remote place reducing public awareness and commotion. Judas's offer permitted them to move up their timetable for arresting and killing Jesus (Stagg, 231).

Preparing for Passover (26:17-19) Preparation for the Passover meal was an extensive undertaking. The Passover meal had to be observed within Jerusalem's city walls. The room in which the Passover was held had to be cleansed of all leaven and any items that might include yeast. A lamb had to be secured and taken to the Temple to be slaughtered by the priests. The lamb was then roasted, and other items for the meal had to be prepared (Boring, 468).

The Passover meal (26:20-25) Jesus tells the disciples that one of them will betray him. None of the disciples seem to suspect

Judas. Instead, they ask, "Is it I?" Perhaps they doubted their own loyalty and were seeking assurance that they were not the guilt1ed for eating, all the disciples were possible candidates. Verse 25, however, indicates that Jesus identified Judas as the betrayer, though perhaps not publicly.

All the disciples except for Judas address Jesus as "Lord"—a term used by followers of Jesus. Judas calls him "Rabbi"—a term used by outsiders (Schweizer, 489).

Verse 24 speaks of both divine sovereignty and human responsibility. The Crucifixion will occur according to God's plan and intentions. Such a reality, however, does not absolve humans of responsibility for their actions. The verse affirms that God is fully sovereign, and humans are fully responsible, both at the same time (Boring, 470).

The cost of betrayal (27:3-10) It is Friday. Judas has betrayed Jesus with a kiss (26:47-50). Jesus has been arrested and turned over to Pilate.

Judas realizes that he has done a horrible thing in betraying Jesus and acknowledges his guilt. He attempts to give back the thirty pieces of silver. The chief priests refuse to accept it. When Judas confessed that he had betrayed an innocent person, by law Jesus' case should have been reconsidered. Judas should have been charged and tried for giving false evidence. But the authorities "have their man" and are not interested in reconsidering anything. In essence, they tell Judas that it's his personal problem and they will have nothing to do with it (Schweizer, 504-505). They had gotten from Judas what they wanted. They did not care what happened to him. At that response, Judas threw down the money, left, and hanged himself.

Matthew is the only Gospel that contains an account of Judas's death. Acts 1:16-20 provides a slightly different account of Judas's death.

Ironically, the ones who totally disregard the law in order to condemn Jesus to death follow the dictates of the law when handling the small amount of money Judas has thrown down. They refuse to put it back into the Temple treasury. According to Deuteronomy 23:18, a verse that strictly refers only to the wages of a female or male prostitute, unclean money cannot be brought into the Lord's house. The chief priests' acknowledgment that the money is unclean indicates their own guilt in this sordid event, for they are the ones who gave the money to Judas. So they decide to use the money to buy a cemetery for foreigners (Jer 18:1-3) (Boring, 484).

Understanding

Matthew provides a contrast of two kingdoms: the Kingdom of God, represented by Jesus, and the kingdom of humankind, represented by Judas. The Kingdom of self-giving is contrasted to the kingdom of selfishness. Giving is contrasted with acquiring, life with death, hope with despair.

This is a story of the betrayal of trust and its consequences. Judas was trusted. He was the treasurer for Jesus and his disciples. He was one of the few whom Jesus chose to teach and with whom Jesus shared his life. Yet he allowed all of Jesus' teachings and actions to fall on an unreceptive heart. Being "close" to Jesus does not guarantee good and holy living.

Judas's betrayal ends in tragedy for all involved. Jesus and Judas both died: one gave his life for others, while the other took his life in utter hopelessness. Evidently, Judas did not think that forgiveness was an option. Although Judas lived so close in proximity to the one who offers forgiveness, he somehow missed it entirely! Judas's story is one of despair winning out over hope.

According to Matthew's account of Judas's story, greed leads us to act in ways that under other circumstances we most likely would not act. Judas sold out for small change. Temptations to make choices that are less than God's intentions for us often look so inviting.

Our motives are seldom pure, our intentions rarely flawless. Judas's motives for betraying Jesus are vague at best. We have hints in Judas's story of the motivating factors at work in his life. Few if any of us act with entirely good or entirely evil motives or intent. Although our motives and intentions are not insignificant, they are not the final, definitive word. Regardless of our motivations and intentions, our actions for good or ill are truly consequential.

When Jesus told the disciples that one of them would betray him, each of them wanted Jesus' assurance that he would not be the one. Perhaps in their quiet moments, they recognized their potential for faithlessness. In fact, when Jesus was arrested, the Scripture indicates that "all the disciples deserted him and fled" (26:56b).

What About Me?

• *Betrayal is a common temptation.* Judas's story is the example we often use for betrayal, but we must remember that all the disciples betrayed Jesus at some level. The phrase Jesus uses at the table, "The one who has dipped his hand into the bowl with me...," points a finger of indictment at us all. How are you tempted to betray Jesus? Have you ever asked the question "Is it I?" Have you been betrayed by a trusted friend, associate, or family member? How did you feel? How did you respond to the betrayal?

• *The cost of betrayal is high.* Judas learns that he has also been betrayed, both by his own lust for power and by the religious leaders. Judas finds himself caught between what he thought he wanted and what he has brought upon himself and Jesus. What are the consequences we face when we sell out our faith, yielding to temptations that cannot deliver what they promise? Judas was used by others for their evil purposes, only to find himself abandoned by them when he realized the gravity of his act. Have you ever experienced a similar occurrence?

• *Motives and intentions are not insignificant, yet our actions may have far-reaching consequences.* Regardless of the exact motivations or reasons for Judas's betrayal, he sold Jesus out for a lesser purpose. Consider your motives and intentions for your actions. How do you examine your motives and sort out your goals when you make decisions?

• *Selfishness leads to despair.* Perhaps Judas's excessive concern for himself allowed him to give Jesus over to the authorities. Soon realizing the gravity of his mistake, Judas gave up in despair.

• *Jesus always offers forgiveness and hope.* The other disciples also betrayed Jesus when they later abandoned him, but they were able to find the hope that Jesus provides. Evidently Judas did not believe that forgiveness was an option for him. But forgiveness is always available. Suicide has been dubbed "a permanent solution to a temporary problem." There is pain in living, but pain can be instructive and redemptive if placed in the hands of our loving God.

Resources

William Barclay, *The Gospel of Matthew*, vol. 2, rev. ed., The Daily Study Bible Series (Philadelphia: Westminster Press, 1975).

M. Eugene Boring, "Matthew," *The New Interpreter's Bible*, ed. Leander E. Keck et al. (Nashville: Abingdon Press, 1995).

Eduard Schweizer, *The Good News According to Matthew*, trans. David E. Green (Atlanta: John Knox Press, 1975).

Frank Stagg, "Matthew," *The Broadman Bible Commentary*: vol. 8, ed. Clifton J. Allen et al. (Nashville: Broadman Press, 1969).

SELLING
OUT

Matthew 26:14-25; 27:3-10

Introduction

Failure can be a powerful teacher. As a disciple, Judas was and remains a failure. He failed to such magnitude until his name has become synonymous with betrayal. The other disciples were ordinary people, but time has made them saints. Today we name our children James, John, Matthew, Philip, Andrew, Peter, and Nathaniel. Do you know any little boy babies being named Judas? Until this day, the name carries a stigma. We don't want to burden a child with that name because it still carries negative freight.

A failure of the magnitude of Judas must have lessons to teach us. Where does this text touch people like you and me? Here are my suggestions.

I. Sin's Consequences are not Predictable.

"Then one of the twelve, who was called Judas Iscariot, went to the chief priests and said, 'What will you give me if I betray him to you?'" (Mt 26:14-15a). Judas took the initiative. A chief priest spy had not tried to catch Judas in a weak moment and seduce him with thirty pieces of silver. It's the other way around. Judas went to them. The phrase "What will you give me..." suggests greed as the motive. Thirty pieces of silver didn't amount to much. "Matthew's quotation refers to silver shekels; at four denarii to the shekel this was one hundred and twenty days' wages" (*The New Oxford Annotated Bible*, New York: Oxford University Press, 1991, 40 NT section). That's not much money for the life of friend.

Perhaps greed was not the motive. What if Judas was trying to force Jesus into a confrontation with the chief priests and the Romans? In that possibility is a hint of something redemptive, even patriotic in what Judas did. He wanted Jesus to lead in the re-establishment of a Jewish kingdom. We know the disciples had this idea earlier in his ministry. If Jesus were thrust before the high priests, then he would have to use his miracle powers to save himself. Pilate and the Romans would be drawn into confrontation. And surely this One who could feed five thousand with five loaves and two fishes could find a way to save himself. These thoughts are speculative, but if they were true, Judas didn't expect Jesus to die.

To lend credibility to my argument, consider Judas's actions when he saw that the plot was leading toward Jesus' death. "When Judas, his betrayer, saw that Jesus was condemned, he repented..." (Mt 27:3) Between the lines I read, "This isn't turning out like I thought it would; it's gone terribly wrong. What have I done?" The sad truth is that "sin's consequences are not predictable." Let me illustrate...

• Do you really think King David anticipated the consequences of his night out with Bathsheba? It was a fit of passion. He thought he could manage the consequence, but the mess multiplied like weeds in a garden. Uriah had to be killed. The baby died. David's good name was tarnished. His children were morally poisoned by the sorry example of their father. David didn't mean for it to get out of hand; but sin is funny that way.

• Do you really think an eighteen year-old who has a couple of beers expects to wreck the family car, seriously hurt his girlfriend, and disappoint his parents? The consequences of what seems like just a little irresponsibility are hard to anticipate. Sometimes the boy and girl are both dead from a thing that seems so small in the moment of decision. The consequences are not innocent. They become deadly and sinful.

• Do you really think the professional who fudged the numbers on his expense account ever imagined what would come of it? Her life was so promising. Every career opportunity opened before her. Travel was demanding. Expenses were pretty much carte blanche. She enjoyed the freedom. The company was doing well. What difference did it make that she padded the numbers a little here and there? Then came the day when everybody's accounts were checked. Her numbers were inflated. She was called to account, dismissed, and fired. She was embarrassed. The next job was hard to find and not nearly so rewarding. Who would have dreamed so small a sin would have such career consequences!

Sin takes on a life of its own. I don't think Judas ever intended for Jesus to die, but "sin's consequences are not predictable."

II. God's Purposes are not Frustrated.

It would seem the betrayal of Jesus might misdirect the designs of God, but not so. "God is not taken by surprise in the betrayal that leads to crucifixion; it goes according to divine plan expressed in Scripture" (M. Eugene Boring, *The New Interpreter's Bible*, Vol. 8, Nashville: Abingdon Press, 1995, 470).

Judas did not catch Jesus by surprise. The other disciples had no inkling of what Judas had done, but Jesus confronts Judas at the Passover meal saying, "Truly I tell you, one of you will betray me" (Mt 26:21). I don't know whether this was the supernatural foreknowledge of God's Son or the keen insight of one who studied each disciple. But Jesus knew what Judas had done and made it plain to Judas that he knew.

I am writing with an assumption that Judas was not wholly wicked. He had a capacity for good. That's why Jesus chose him to be among the twelve. Judas must have felt down and dirty when Jesus said, "The one who has dipped his hand into the bowl with me will betray me. The Son of Man goes as it is written of him, but woe to that one by whom the Son of Man is betrayed!" (Mt 26:23-24). This text makes a distinction we need to note:
• "The Son of Man goes as it is written of him." God's intention for Jesus was not derailed, cut short, or frustrated by the treachery of Judas. Salvation came by means of the cross no matter what Judas did. We may complicate God's plans, but we never frustrate them. Judas did not keep Jesus from accomplishing what God sent him to do.

• "But woe to that one by whom the Son of Man is betrayed!" Even though Judas' actions bent to God's purposes, Judas was still responsible for his wicked deed. God turned wickedness for good, but our wickedness is still wickedness no matter that God makes good come of it.

So Matthew would say of Judas, "It would have been better for that one not to have been born" (Mt 26:24b). Some sins are worse than others.

III. Some Choices are not Retrievable.

Matthew is the only gospel to follow the Judas subplot to its ugly end. Judas led "a large crowd with swords and clubs, from the chief priests and the elders of the people" to the Garden of Gethsemane (Mt 26:47). Judas kissed Jesus to identify him as the one to be arrested. Trials followed and Judas was near enough to know what was happening. When Jesus was condemned an alarm went off in Judas's cloudy brain. "This has gotten out of hand. I've got to do something to try to save a desperate situation." Note how he did all the right things:
• "He repented..." (27:3a).
• He "brought back the thirty pieces of silver to the chief priests and the elders" (27:3b).
• "He said, 'I have sinned by betraying innocent blood'" (27:4).

Judas had a conscience. His soul was not dead. He had ideas of the enormity of his sin. He doing everything in his power to retrieve his mistake. It's as if he were a child in the school-yard saying to a friend, "I take it back."

It is poor theology to reason that if I say, "I'm sorry," God is beholden to offer grace. God has to forgive me. I said the magic words. If that be so, didn't Judas do all the right things? Why could he not pick up where he left off?

Next week's lesson is about Simon Peter. Peter denied Jesus three times, but he was restored. In fact, Peter was elevated to a high place among the apostles. What's the difference in what Peter did and what Judas did? One denied Jesus; the other betrayed Jesus. Is there all that much difference between the two?

Eugene Boring gives good guidance to such questions.

From Matthew's point of view, what Judas lacks and what Peter has is that fundamental reorientation from the kingdom of this world, represented by thinking human things, to the kingdom represented by Jesus ("thinking divine things"; cf. 16:21-23). ...For Matthew, the story becomes another expression of the conflict of kingdoms, an illustration of how terrible it is to cast one's lot with the wrong side (12:25-30) (Boring, *The New Interpreter's Bible*, Vol. 8. 484).

Judas makes a powerful point: Grace is neither cheap nor automatic. Some things you can't get back.
• If a parent wastes the time when children are small, they can't get it back. It does not matter how sorry they are or how much they try to make it up to the child. The time is lost.
• If you are lazy in college, rarely can you go back and do serious time in college. You may learn from your error, but you can't get back the time.
• If I squander the trust of my wife by a dalliance with another, my wife may continue to live in my house but she will not trust me again as she did before. My saying I am sorry will not restore the trust of young love.

Judas makes the point. Some things can't be retrieved. It does not matter how penitent we are or how much we try to "do the right thing."
The chief priests would not help Judas undo his betrayal. Jesus would die. Judas saw no way out. The text simply, brutally says, "he went out and hanged himself" (Mt 27:5b). So ended a life that had a chance to be something very good.
We still have choices. This lesson can be a warning. Let's learn from his failure. The application of this text is in the outline.
(1) Sin's consequences are not predictable.
(2) God's purposes are not frustrated.
(3) Some choices are not retrievable.

Notes

Notes

3

FAITH AND TEMPTATION

Matthew 26:36-46

Central Question

How do we remain faithful when tempted?

Scripture

Matthew 26:36-46 Then Jesus went with them to a place called Gethsemane; and he said to his disciples, "Sit here while I go over there and pray." 37 He took with him Peter and the two sons of Zebedee, and began to be grieved and agitated. 38 Then he said to them, "I am deeply grieved, even to death; remain here, and stay awake with me." 39 And going a little farther, he threw himself on the ground and prayed, "My Father, if it is possible, let this cup pass from me; yet not what I want but what you want." 40 Then he came to the disciples and found them sleeping; and he said to Peter, "So, could you not stay awake with me one hour? 41 Stay awake and pray that you may not come into the time of trial; the spirit indeed is willing, but the flesh is weak." 42 Again he went away for the second time and prayed, "My Father, if this cannot pass unless I drink it, your will be done." 43 Again he came and found them sleeping, for their eyes were heavy. 44 So leaving them again, he went away and prayed for the third time, saying the same words. 45 Then he came to the disciples and said to them, "Are you still sleeping and taking your rest? See, the hour is at hand, and the Son of Man is betrayed into the hands of sinners. 46 Get up, let us be going. See, my betrayer is at hand."

Remembering

Jesus has finished the Passover meal with the disciples, breaking the bread and sharing the cup. Judas has arranged to betray Jesus to the chief priests, who have decided that Jesus must die.

At the Passover meal, Jesus told the disciples "Truly I tell you, one of you will betray me" (26:21). This news greatly distresses the disciples. They have followed Jesus for almost three years. They love Jesus, although they do not always understand him. They "began to say to him one after another, 'Surely not I, Lord?'" (26:22). Jesus assures them that the disciple who dips into the common bowl with him will be the one who betrays him. Judas responds, "Surely not I, Rabbi?" (26:25) By referring to Jesus as "Rabbi" (in Matthew, a term used by those who don't believe) instead of "Lord" (a term used by those who do believe), Judas reveals that he is the one (Schweizer, 489).

Jesus tells the disciples that they will all desert him (26:31). Peter, however, assures Jesus that even if all the others desert him, he will not do so. Jesus tells Peter that he will deny him. In protest, Peter says that even if he must die with Jesus, he will not deny him. All the disciples agree that they will not deny Jesus.

Immediately following the events in our Scripture text, Jesus is betrayed by Judas and arrested. He is taken to the high priest's house, where Peter does, in fact, deny him three times.

It is a night of temptation. Jesus, Judas, and the rest of the disciples face various temptations in the darkness of this night. How they respond will clarify their faith.

In our text, Jesus has a final opportunity to turn away from the cross and take an easier route. Instead, in the midst of great pain and grief, Jesus uses this opportunity to gather the necessary resources to face his death.

Studying

The garden (26:36) The word *Gethsemane* means "oil-press" or "olive vat." The place was an enclosed garden or orchard.

The term "with" occurs in verses 36, 38, and 40 of this chapter indicating the bond that Jesus had *with* his disciples. In verse 36, Jesus "went with them." In verses 38 and 40, he asks the disciples to remain "with him." Like almost everyone who faces a great challenge, Jesus deeply yearns for companionship and support.

> Old olive trees still stand about three-fourths of a mile east of Jerusalem. Although no one is certain, this site may have been the garden of Gethsemane. the very place where Jesus struggled with his future (Robertson, 211).

The disciples (26:37-38) Leaving the remaining disciples, Jesus takes Peter, James, and John, the same group of disciples present at the Transfiguration (19:1), deeper into the garden. These three had also claimed that they were prepared to die with Jesus (20:22, 26:35).

Jesus is "grieved" and "agitated." Loss always accompanies grief. Jesus' losses are many, his death imminent. His disciples will betray, deny, and abandon him. He has striven to teach those around him of God's great redemptive care for all creation. His disciples' understanding is mixed at best, and now the "window of opportunity" is gone.

In order to reemphasize the depth of his pain, Jesus speaks plainly. His sorrow is as bad as it can get. Jesus describes it as the grief of death.

Jesus asks the disciples to "stay awake." Besides admonishing them not to sleep, Jesus calls the disciples to be alert, to be sensitive to the situation that confronts all of them. These are defining moments for both Jesus and the disciples. Unless all are alert, they will fail God, each other, and themselves.

Jesus' decision (26:39-43) Even though his closest friends are nearby, this decision is one only he can make, so he moves a little distance from the three. Revealed in these few verses is the honest struggle of the divine and also human Jesus. Though he does not want to die, he places his future in the hands of a loving and merciful God.

Meanwhile, the disciples have failed to provide the human support and companionship Jesus needed. They have fallen asleep. The "you" in the question Jesus asks them, "So, could you not stay awake with me one hour?" is plural, which means that Jesus is addressing all three disciples rather than Peter alone (Schweizer, 493).

Once again Jesus admonishes the three to stay awake, be alert. This time, however, he asks them to do it, not only because he needs support and companionship, but also that they might gather necessary spiritual resources. In the very near future, they will need strength to remain faithful in the face of a great temptation.

Jesus again separates himself from the disciples. Jesus' prayer moves from seeking deliverance from death "to trust and commitment to God's will, using the identical words he had taught his disciples in 6:10" (Boring, 477). Through prayer, Jesus was able to withstand the temptation not to follow the will of God. His praying becomes the example and the "basis for all praying in the community" of faith (Schweizer, 493-494).

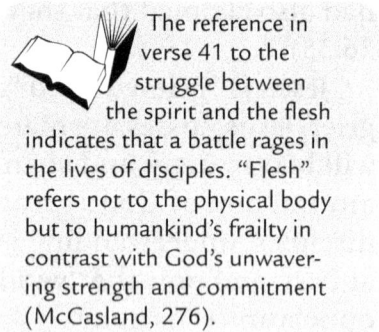

The reference in verse 41 to the struggle between the spirit and the flesh indicates that a battle rages in the lives of disciples. "Flesh" refers not to the physical body but to humankind's frailty in contrast with God's unwavering strength and commitment (McCasland, 276).

The time is at hand (26:43-46) For the third time, Jesus returns to find the disciples sleeping. This time he doesn't bother to awaken them, apparently giving up on having their support. So he leaves them and prays a third time, "saying the same words" in his prayer. "Jesus' three prayers form a dramatic contrast to the three denials of Peter, who sleeps instead of praying" (Boring, 477).

Through prayer, Jesus has gathered the necessary spiritual strength to embrace God's will. With the phrase "The time is at hand," Jesus announces Judas's arrival. These same words, however, also suggest the imminent arrival of God's Kingdom through Jesus' death and resurrection. Evidently Jesus sees or hears Judas and those who will arrest him. He has sought the support of his disciples. He has sought to teach them how to follow in his footsteps. They have failed him three times. So, rejecting the violent reaction of one of his own disciples (26:52), criticizing those who came to capture him because they carried weapons (26:55), and submitting himself to God's will, offering no resistance he steps forward to go with the crowd who came for him (Jn 10:17-18; 18:11).

Understanding

Usually when we think of a "garden," we think of a quiet and peaceful place. On this Thursday evening before the Crucifixion, however, this garden was the place of incredible turmoil, grief, and temptation. Jesus had several options. He could have chosen to escape before Judas arrived. To anyone who enjoyed life as much as Jesus, that had to be an attractive option. He could have chosen to fall asleep like the disciples. Another option was for him to accept his death with a self-righteous attitude, "blaming it on the 'generation of vipers,' as [John] the Baptist had done" (Kunkel, 260). Jesus knew, however, that any of these options would have been contrary to God's will for him.

This text speaks of Jesus' need for companionship during crisis. He chose those closest to him to serve as a source of strength. Having friends present to help us face our most diffi-cult days can be immeasurably helpful even if we must face the temptation alone. When Jesus needed companionship the most, however, he had it the least. His friends were tired and completely unaware of imminent tragedy.

Remaining alert to the times, to our situation, and to what is happening is critical if we are to yield successfully to God's will. The disciples fell asleep; they did not follow Jesus' example. Subsequently, they did not have the resources to follow him to the cross, even though they had proclaimed their willingness to die with him.

Nothing in the text indicates that God spoke to Jesus. There is no ministering angel, no disciple, no voice to comfort and encourage Jesus (Marney, 26). Although we should not make too much out of the silence of the text on this point, an important question is raised. How can we continue to be faithful when we get no strong and evident word from God about our situation? Jesus was able to do it because he had lived his whole life following God's will. It was a natural progression for him to continue, based on what he sensed his calling to be. Even when Jesus does not sense the nearness of God, he continues to remain faithful with the promise and hope that God will redeem the situation.

Jesus is clearly no passive bystander to the final events of his life. Through prayer, he finds the spiritual strength to walk faithfully and confidently into God's future. Jesus takes an active role in stepping towards the pain and death that is to follow. Judas and those who come with him do not find Jesus surprised or reluctant to go with them.

What About Me?

• *All of us have struggled with God's will for our lives.* The journey through Gethsemane represents a time of intense struggle for Jesus. His grief is overwhelming, and he asks his closest friends for support. They do not provide it. When have you asked your friends for support during a difficult time? When have your friends let you down? Are you available and "present" for those who need you in their hours of trial and temptation? How can we help each other remain faithful in the face of temptation?

• *Struggle and grief can help us move towards faithful living instead of towards yielding to temptation.* While his friends slept, Jesus agonized over his life, mission, and future. Jesus prayed to God for help. Why and how do you pray?

• *Prayer is a necessary component of finding God's direction.* Jesus spoke of the value and need for prayer. He modeled his belief by praying a portion of the Lord's Prayer in the face of his fiercest temptation. What temptations invite you to live outside of God's intentions? How do you confront them? By faithful, alert praying? By sleeping?

• *God's direction is sometimes hard to accept.* In verse 42, Jesus prays, "...if this cannot pass unless I drink it, your will be done." When have you submitted to God's will? Do you need to submit to God's will?

• *Faithful living results in faithful responses in the face of trial and temptation.* From the silence of the garden arises the voice of Jesus. Without his friends, seemingly without God, Jesus' faith is the only clear voice in this text: "Not my will...but yours." Having practiced a life of faith, Jesus' plea to God comes naturally as the only expression he could make. When has your faith enabled you to face the future, determined to follow God's will, regardless of the consequences?

No testing has overtaken you that is not common to everyone. God is faithful, and he will not let you be tested beyond your strength, but with the testing he will also provide the way out so that you may be able to endure it (1 Corinthians 10:13-14). Blessed is anyone who endures temptation. Such a one has stood the test and will receive the crown of life that the Lord has promised to those who love him. No one, when tempted, should say, "I am being tempted by God"; for God cannot be tempted by evil and he himself tempts no one. But one is tempted by one's own desire, being lured and enticed by it; then, when that desire has conceived, it gives birth to sin, and that sin, when it is fully grown, gives birth to death (James 1:12-15).

Resources

Twelve Steps of Alcoholics Anonymous, *aa.org* <www.aa.org/default/en_about_aa_sub.cfm? subpageid=76&pageid=12> (25 November 2002).

FAITH AND TEMPTATION

Matthew 26:36-46

Introduction

This lesson is about struggling with faith. Any glib references to the humanity of Jesus should fall away in the power and awe of this lesson. William Barclay opened his comment on our text with this line: "Surely this is a passage which we must approach upon our knees" (*The Gospel of Matthew*, Vol. II, Philadelphia: Westminster Press, 1958 edition, 384).

The public ministry of Jesus had temptations for bookends. It began with a severe testing in the Judean wilderness. Satan tempted Jesus to misuse his powers. "Command these stones to become loaves of bread" (Mt 4:3b). At the end of his ministry, Jesus is in the Garden of Gethsemane struggling with all it meant to be Jesus, the Lamb of God, the Son of God. The temptation to turn away from it all and run had to be real. The nearer we come to "doing the will of God," the more attention the Devil gives us. Jesus took much of the Devil's time.

I. He Was Hurting; He Wanted Support, 26:36-38.

Jesus was God's Son, a miracle-worker. He was sinless. These teachings are true and have value for our spiritual formation. There is, however, a subtle temptation built into this theology. The temptation runs like this: "Jesus is divine. Jesus is so different from you and me until he is on a totally different plane. His temptations were easily avoided and his pains were not real."

This text reveals that Jesus' humanity was as real as his divinity. His pain was as real as ours. This verse can be especially helpful to understanding the Gethsemane text: "For we do not have a high priest who is unable to sympathize with our weaknesses, but we have one who in every respect has been tested as we are, yet without sin" (Heb 4:15). To interpret Gethsemane correctly, we need to take Hebrews 4:15 to heart.

This is the text's setting:
• It is Thursday night. In a couple of hours, Judas will come with high priests and soldiers. The end will begin.
• Jesus has just shared the Lord's Supper with his disciples. The eleven have retired to the Garden of Gethsemane.
• Jesus tells eight disciples to wait. He invites Peter, James, and John further into the garden. These three witnessed the Transfiguration.

The humanity of Jesus is revealed in two poignant ways.

(1) He was hurting. "Then he said to them (Peter, James and John), 'I am deeply grieved, even to death...' And going a little further, he threw himself on the ground and prayed..." (Mt 26:38-39a). Another translation powerfully catches the emotion. "Then he began to be full of anguish and distress, and he said to them, 'My soul is crushed with anguish to the point of death...'" (Weymouth, *The New Testament in Modern Speech*, Boston: The Pilgrim Press, 1943, 71).

Why was Jesus hurting? Here are my speculations:
• Fear of immediate and horrible death. It was staring him in the face. Jesus' death would not be painless. It would be calculated agony.
• Fear of failure. Sherman Johnson commented, "By all human standards his mission had failed" (Johnson, *The Interpreter's Bible*, Vol. 7, New York: Abingdon Press, 1951, 579).
• Fear that he couldn't go through with it. I think Jesus was ambiguous about his own strength. I see it as a kind of self-doubt. He was saying, "I know what I'm supposed to do; I don't know if I can do it." Further, I don't think this idea controlled him. It was in his mind. It was his worst fear.

(2) He needed support. "Then he said to them... 'remain here and stay awake with me'" (Mt 26:38). My perspective as pastor may be helpful. As their pastor, my congregations have seen me as a caregiver. I visited hospitals, talked with people about their troubles, and counseled congregations in sermons. But

sometimes, I needed care and support only the people of my congregations could give. When we discovered Dot had cancer, the congregation supported the caregiver. When Daddy died, the congregation generously gave their support. I was supposed to be their support; they became mine.

We think of Jesus as always being the one who gave help, but this time Jesus asked for support. "Remain here, and stay awake with me" (Mt 26:38b). It is a pity that when Jesus needed help, the disciples were too tired to give it. Loneliness is the shadow that darkens the edges of this text. Jesus asked for support a second time. He didn't get it (26:40).

It would seem that the disciples could have sensed how much Jesus needed them. Judging the disciples as weak or insensitive is easy, but it's not fair. As Jesus was human in asking support, so the disciples were human in falling asleep.

It should not seem strange that Jesus needs our support. Does Jesus need our support caring for the Church? Does Jesus need our support teaching children? Does Jesus need our support when a bright youth enters the ministry? Generously Jesus has given of himself for us. Generously we must respond by supporting his call, his teachings, his Church. Support is always a two-way street.

II. Two Parts of Jesus Were Pulling at Each Other, 26:39-42.

In this case, and following the lead of Matthew who quoted Jesus, "the spirit indeed is willing, but the flesh is weak" (26:41b), two parts will refer to spirit and flesh. The high point in our text is in the twice-spoken prayer of Jesus "My Father, if it is possible, let this cup pass from me; yet not what I want but what you want" (Mt 26:39b). After speaking with the disciples, he prayed again, "My Father, if this cannot pass unless I drink it, your will be done" (Mt 26:42b). In this prayer:

(1) Jesus is earnestly appealing for a way out. Can I be spared dying? Is there any other way? Does this have to be? Is this what you require of me?

Some have said, "God would not ask that of anyone," especially when something with extreme difficulty is asked, great suffering is expected, and social rejection is involved. Ultimately,

God would have the victory, but the world is hard on God's chosen.

(2) Jesus is always submissive to God's will. Both times the prayer for release is coupled with "not what I want but what you want" and "your will be done." This submissiveness is the wonder, the glory of Jesus. Paul wrote of Jesus' glory:

> Let the same mind be in you that was in Christ Jesus,
> who, though he was in the form of God,
> did not regard equality with God
> as something to be exploited,
> but emptied himself,
> taking the form of a slave,
> being born in human likeness.
> And being found in human form,
> he humbled himself
> and became obedient to the point of death—
> even death on the cross.
> Therefore God also highly exalted him...(Phil 2:5-9).

Jesus followed God's will though it cost him his life. That is his glory. All Christian sacrifice is now measured by Gethsemane and Calvary. Doing "God's will" may involve much more than a monetary gift, taking an assignment at the church, or making a two-week mission trip. These are good things, but they are at a lower level of dedication than Gethsemane and Calvary. Jesus struggled when he faced death in God's service, but he was true to himself. Earlier in his ministry, Jesus had said of himself, "My food is to do the will of him who sent me and to complete his work" (Jn 4:34).

Could the divine and the human war inside Jesus? Matthew's text suggests that they can. "The spirit indeed is willing, but the flesh is weak" (Mt 26:41b). It is not possible for us to understand the personality of One who was fully divine *and* fully human. But we do have some insight. I am part divine and part human. God is my Father *and* I come of earthly parents. Do spirit and flesh struggle in me? Too often. Could it be that the fully human Jesus was crying out to be heard in the Garden prayer? This might account for the anguish and turmoil of it all.

III. Time is Up; Let's do the Right Thing, 26:45-46.

Almost abruptly, Matthew ends the Garden prayer. The disciples could not keep from sleeping. Jesus has prayed, begging for escape from the cross. He has ended his prayer offering himself in submission to God's will. Judas and the soldiers were on their way. Contemplation had to end. The horrible action of the cross interrupted the private agony of the Garden. Life is always that way. Prayer steeled Jesus for what was to come. "See, the hour is at hand, and the Son of Man is betrayed into the hands of sinners. Get up, let us be going. See, my betrayer is at hand" (Mt 26:45b-46). Suddenly, Jesus was no longer pleading with God for release. He was ready.

• "The hour is at hand." There is no more time for teaching or explaining. The climax of Jesus' mission on earth is at hand. For this reason, Jesus was born.

• "The Son of Man is betrayed into the hands of sinners." Jesus didn't say, "Something bad might happen." He said his betrayal was to happen now!

• The tone of Matthew's account leaves no doubt about Jesus' resolve. All that was shaky or unsure when Jesus prayed has been settled.

Often, when facing hard things, we become confused. We struggle in our own private Gethsemane. When we come out on the other side, we are settled and committed. In all our Gethsemane times, we have something Jesus didn't have. We have an example. I doubt any of us will go to a cross, but we will have hard testing both morally and physically. My prayer is that after Gethsemane, we are full of courage, strength, and are able to be a good witness...like Jesus.

Notes

Notes

4

FAILURE AND FORGIVENESS

Matthew 26:57-58, 69-75

Central Question

Do we find forgiveness in light of our failure?

Scripture

Matthew 26:57-58 Those who had arrested Jesus took him to Caiaphas the high priest, in whose house the scribes and the elders had gathered. 58 But Peter was following him at a distance, as far as the courtyard of the high priest; and going inside, he sat with the guards in order to see how this would end.

Matthew 26:69-75 Now Peter was sitting outside in the courtyard. A servant-girl came to him and said, "You also were with Jesus the Galilean." 70 But he denied it before all of them, saying, "I do not know what you are talking about." 71 When he went out to the porch, another servant-girl saw him, and she said to the bystanders, "This man was with Jesus of Nazareth." 72 Again he denied it with an oath, "I do not know the man." 73 After a little while the bystanders came up and said to Peter, "Certainly you are also one of them, for your accent betrays you." 74 Then he began to curse, and he swore an oath, "I do not know the man!" At that moment the cock crowed. 75 Then Peter remembered what Jesus had said: "Before the cock crows, you will deny me three times." And he went out and wept bitterly.

Remembering

Peter was one of Jesus' first followers. He is first introduced as Simon. According to John 1:41-42, Andrew, Peter's brother, introduced him to Jesus. When Jesus met Simon, he told him that from that moment on, he would be called Peter, which means "rock."

The New Testament records many examples of Peter's living up to the name Jesus gave him. Throughout Jesus' ministry, people were puzzled by Jesus. They were constantly trying to figure out exactly what kind of person he was. On one occasion when Jesus was talking with his disciples about his identity, he asked them, "But who do you say that I am?" (Mt 16:15). Peter then offered the insightful confession, "You are the Messiah, the Son of the living God" (Mt 16:16).

Later, before Jesus shared his last meal with the disciples, he began washing the disciples' feet. Peter resisted, saying, "You will never wash my feet!" (Jn 13:9). But when Jesus indicated the necessity of this act of service, Peter quickly asked Jesus to wash him from head to toe!

The Scriptures for today's lesson record events that took place on Thursday evening before Good Friday. Jesus meets with his disciples for the Passover meal. He identifies Judas as the one who will betray him. Additionally, he warns Peter that "before the cock crows, you will deny me three times" (26:34). In predictable fashion, Peter assures Jesus in no uncertain terms that he is prepared to die for, not deny, Jesus. Immediately following this exchange, Jesus walks to Gethsemane to pray, taking Peter, James, and John with him. During their time in Gethsemane, Judas arrives and betrays Jesus, and Jesus is arrested. According to John 18:10, Peter takes out his sword to defend Jesus and cuts off an ear of one of the slaves of the high priest. But the incident ends with these words: "Then all the disciples deserted him and fled" (26:56b).

All four Gospels include the story of Peter's denial. "The church's honesty in exposing the failings of its heroes is a healthy self-criticism. The saints are yet sinners and concede it. No effort is made to excuse Peter's failure" (Stagg, 240).

Studying

Out in the yard (26:57-58) According to Matthew, Peter doesn't flee far. He follows at a distance. Following at a distance is not necessarily more faithful than totally abandoning Jesus as the rest of the disciples did. Peter's curiosity, not his faith, takes him to the home of the high priest, Caiaphas. He wants to see what will happen, how this incident will play out. Peter's action, however, is not without significant courage. Just being present in such a hostile environment is potentially dangerous, for the assumption is that Jesus will be executed (Stagg, 240). Peter positions himself with the guards in the courtyard, on the outer edge of transpiring events.

Identified (26:69-70) While Peter is sitting in the courtyard, a female servant accuses him of being one of Jesus' followers. She speaks only to Peter. In response to her accusation, Peter denies it "before all of them" (verse 70a). His reply is vague and evasive. He pretends not to know what she is talking about. Perhaps if he feigns ignorance, he can avoid a nasty situation. The servant uses the term "Jesus the Galilean." "Galilean" is used derogatorily. "It may have suggested that he was a potential revolutionary" (Schweizer, 500).

I never knew him (26:71-72) Surely trying to avoid another confrontation, Peter moves to the porch, farther out on the edge where there is less light. Yet no escape seems available for him. Another female servant speaks, not to Peter, but to those standing around her. She, too, accuses Peter of following Jesus. This time Peter is not evasive. He categorically denies even knowing Jesus. He uses an oath to underscore his denial. Peter's oath is probably similar to our saying "so help me God" after a statement in order to underscore its truth.

> "Again, you have heard that it was said to those of ancient times, 'You shall not swear falsely, but carry out the vows you have made to the Lord.' But I say to you, Do not swear at all, either by heaven, for it is the throne of God, or by the earth, for it is his footstool, or by Jerusalem, for it is the city of the great King. And do not swear by your head, for you cannot make one hair white or black. Let your word be 'Yes, Yes' or 'No, No'; anything more than this comes from the evil one" (Matthew 5:3-37).

In the Sermon on the Mount (5:33-37), Jesus had told his followers to be truthful and forthright in their statements to each other. His followers are to live transparently faithful lives, both in word and deed. There is no need for oaths, for they change nothing. With his second denial, Peter "digs a bigger hole" for himself. Peter covers one lie with a bigger one.

Instead of using the derogatory phrase "the Galilean," in Matthew 26:71 the second girl refers to Jesus as "Jesus of Nazareth." This is the first such reference since Matthew 2:23.

Final denial (26:73-74) Finally Peter is confronted by the bystanders to whom the second female servant had made her comment. Peter's second denial had given him away. "From his speech it was clear that he was a Galilean. The Galileans spoke with a burr; so ugly was their accent that no Galilean was allowed to pronounce the benediction at a synagogue service" (Barclay, 346). These bystanders tell him that his accent indicates that he is one of Jesus' followers. Although Peter had previously said, "Even though I must die *with* you, I will not deny you" (26:35), he has now three times been accused of associating *with* Jesus.

Peter's third denial is loud and emphatic. He uses profanity plus an oath in maintaining that he does "not know the man!" This is the only time the Greek word for "curse" is used in the New Testament. According to one scholar, the text "suggests that Peter cursed Jesus" (Boring, 481). Once again, he has to cover a lie with a bigger one.

The rooster crows (26:75) The rooster crows and Peter remembers what Jesus had said. Peter would betray Jesus three times before the rooster crowed. Peter is filled with remorse and begins to weep.

This story is marked by several contrasts. In the verses preceding our Scripture text, Jesus found strength for his impending confrontation by

engaging three times in prayer at Gethsemane. Peter fell asleep three times in Gethsemane. Now he denies Jesus three times. Jesus stood firm in the face of the probing of the high priest. Peter collapses when confronted by the high priest's servant. Jesus refused to use an oath to underscore the truth of his statements. Now Peter not only uses an oath, but also adds profanity (Boring, 481).

Understanding

Among the disciples, Peter was a leader. He had insight that other disciples lacked. He was bold in his affirmations of faith. He told Jesus that he was prepared to die with him. He was certain that Jesus could count on him in difficult situations.

One can almost hear the pride in his voice when he said to Jesus, "Though all become deserters because of you, I will never desert you" (Mt 26:33). Nonetheless, "pride goes before destruction, and a haughty spirit before a fall" (Prov 16:18). Just as boldly and publicly as he had professed his faith, Peter failed to be faithful at a critical point.

Being a faithful disciple of Jesus is a daily challenge. In the midst of unanticipated events and inattentive moments, temptations from within us and around us can lead us toward faithlessness. Our strengths can sometimes be great weaknesses, often because we think we consider ourselves not susceptible to failure. Pride in spiritual accomplishments can leave us vulnerable to big failures, as Peter's denial so poignantly reminds us.

The proverbial statement "honesty *is* the best policy" is good advice. "Aristotle said that the penalty of telling a lie is that the liar is not believed when he tells the truth" (Buttrick, 590). Peter's first denial (or lie) was a mere evasion, "I don't know what you are talking about" (Mt 26:70b). His second denial was forthright, including a prohibited oath: "I do not know the man" (26:72b). His third and final denial included an oath and profanity. Peter's experience exemplifies the "downward spiral" of lying. On each occasion, he had to tell a greater lie in order to cover the earlier one. It seems an easily avoided mistake when reading about it later, but in a moment of "battle" it is easy to forget. Simple honesty and integrity are kingdom virtues. If we cannot be counted on to be truthful about minor things, how can we expect to be believed in anything we say?

Fear was no doubt one of the motivating factors in Peter's three denials. His pride and his fear led him to take the precise course of action he had said he would never take. He feared for his life. Our lives may not be in jeopardy, but we nonetheless face fear. We may fear what others say about us, what others might do to us—professionally, personally, corporately. Fear can and does move us to act like cowards.

Our only hope is the love, mercy, and forgiveness of God. Peter's story of redemption, which follows this incident, is not included in our text today. Peter's relationship with God was restored, and he later became one of the stalwart leaders of the early Christian church. He could do nothing to "dig" himself out of the hole in which he found himself. But the risen Christ forgave him, even his denials, and restored him to spiritual health and Christian leadership.

What About Me?

• *Fear is a powerful motivater.* Peter allowed his fear to overcome his loyalty and his faith. Curiosity seemed the primary driving force behind his coming to the courtyard. Once caught by the questions of a slave girl, his curiosity turns to denial. What fears control you? Do you fear what others may say about you if you are faithful to Christ?

Peter made the mistake of following Jesus "at a distance" (verse 58a). How closely do you seek to follow Jesus? Does fear, pride, or something else keep you at a distance from real and serious discipleship?

• *Let your "yes" be "yes" and your "no" be "no."* Jesus teaches us to live with integrity and honesty. Our words should be so consistent that their veracity is unquestionable. Do you consistently speak the truth?

• *Faithful living is a daily discipline.* The crowing rooster reminds Peter of Jesus' words. It must have been one of those rare moments when everything becomes painfully clear. Peter was reminded of his own words of loyalty, Jesus' insightful words of discernment, and Peter's actions. At that moment, Peter was faced with a great lesson of discipleship: it is a day-by-day and moment-by-moment process.

• *Our greatest strengths can become the source of our greatest weakness.* What are your greatest strengths? Have you ever thought that your strengths, because of pride, might actually be points where you are susceptible to temptation?

• *In the hands of God, even our greatest failures can be used for great things.* Peter's experience reminds us that our failure doesn't have to be final. Though Peter had placed himself in a great hole of his own digging, God was able to raise him again to level ground. From this vantage point, Peter was able to accept his own failure and embrace Christ's forgiveness. Are you stuck at the point of your failures and unable to move beyond them? Peter's story reminds us that there is hope. As later Scripture shows, Peter was able to accept Christ's forgiveness and become one who offered that forgiveness to others. Have you been able to make this movement?

Resources

William Barclay, "The Gospel of Matthew", vol. 2: Rev. Edition, *The Daily Study Bible Series* (Philadelphia: Westminster Press, 1975).

M. Eugene Boring, "Matthew," *The New Interpreter's Bible*, ed. Leander E. Keck et al. (Nashville: Abingdon Press, 1995).

George A. Buttrick, "Matthew," *The Interpreter's Bible*, ed. George A. Buttrick, et al. (Nashville: Abingdon Press, 1951).

Eduard Schweizer, *The Good News According to Matthew*, trans. David E. Green (Atlanta: John Knox Press, 1975).

Frank Stagg, "Matthew," *The Broadman Bible Commentary, Vol. 8*, ed. Clifton J. Allen et al. (Nashville: Broadman Press, 1969).

FAILURE AND FORGIVENESS

Matthew 26:57-58, 69-75

Introduction

Two weeks ago, we studied the sad story of Judas's betrayal of Jesus. Did Judas find forgiveness? We don't know and we can't find the answers in this life. We can learn lessons from failure, but they are hard lessons. Hope lies in warning.

Today's lesson is different. Judas did an awful thing. Peter did an awful thing. Judas was overtaken with guilt and shame. He tried to make things right, but he couldn't change the consequences. He took his life. Peter was so embarrassed by his sin of denial he "went out and wept bitterly" (Mt 26:75b). For reasons only God knows fully, Peter was forgiven and given a large responsibility in the Church and her mission. Peter's sin did not end his future or his calling. God's grace was with Peter. He became the leader of the apostles, a first witness to the resurrection, and the preacher at Pentecost.

For reasons that are obvious, this lesson is more appealing than our study of Judas. Most people will have no trouble finding themselves in this story. Learning that God uses people who disappoint God and themselves will be good news. There is a sense in which this story is everyone's story. We've all said we would not deny Jesus...but we have. And we are still trying to follow Christ. I still don't want to deny Jesus. How can I keep my promises? How can I keep from being somebody I don't want to be?

I. Honesty: The New Testament does not protect her heroes.

Most scholars agree that Peter was the primary source for Mark. Mark was the source for Matthew. In fact, Mark's gospel can be interpreted as the sermons of Peter. This means Peter gave us this story.

All four Gospels record Peter's denial of Jesus. The evidence suggests that Peter used his story in his sermons regularly. He didn't try to hide what he had done. He was like Paul in that he began his sermons autobiographically. When Paul was arrested in Jerusalem, this is how he began his defense:

> I am a Jew, born in Tarsus in Cilicia, but brought up in this city at the feet of Gamaliel, educated strictly according to our ancestral law, being zealous for God, just as all of you are today. I persecuted this Way up to the point of death by binding both men and women and putting them in prison, as the high priest and the whole council of elders can testify about me....While I was on my way and approaching Damascus, about noon a great light from heaven suddenly shone about me...(Acts 22:3-6).

Paul learned from Peter to use his personal experiences to demonstrate the grace of God. Almost hidden in Galatians are autobiographical details that bind Peter and Paul. After Paul's conversion, he did not confer with anyone. He retired to Arabia for three years; "then after three years I did go up to Jerusalem to visit Cephas and stayed with him fifteen days; I did not see any other apostle except James the Lord's brother" (Gal 1:17-19). The point of this lengthy illustration is that Paul learned both his theology and his method from Peter. Peter taught him by word and example not to hide his former sins. They were not to present themselves as wonderful, perfect, examples of Christian faith. They were to point to a Savior who forgives people who do bad things. God uses those people as illustrations of the forgiving grace of Christ and as useful servants to enlarge the Kingdom.

Keep these two ideas in mind:

(1) Have confidence in the Scripture. Sometimes the tiny details don't fit, but the sense of the sacred text is always trustworthy. The biblical saints did not have the advantage of public relations "spin." Peter and Paul are both honored as great

servants of God, but they were not spared the exposure of their sins. Their sins are out for us to see.

(2) Recognize the grace of God. Even the best evangels were once sorry examples of faith. Both Peter and Paul used their sins to illustrate the grace of God. If Christ can transform and use Peter and Paul, maybe he can do something with you and me...that's the message.

II. Humility: "Though all become deserters because of you, I will never desert you" (Mt 26:33).

Peter is reputed as a brash leader. He had few thoughts he did not speak. The picture the gospels paint of him is mixed.
• On Lake Galilee, Jesus came to the disciples "walking on the sea" (Mt 14:25). The disciples were not sure it was Jesus and they were frightened. Jesus said, "Take heart, it is I; do not be afraid" (14:27). Peter said, "Lord if it is you, command me to come to you on the water" (14:28). Jesus did. Peter began to walk on the water just like Jesus. Unfortunately, that's not the end of the story. When Peter "noticed the strong wind, he became frightened, and beginning to sink, he cried out, 'Lord, save me!'" (14:30). This incident encapsulates Peter's character. He was quick to speak (the other disciples are silent). He was not afraid to ask Jesus for special privileges (may I walk on water, too?). But Peter's faith was shaky.
• Late in his ministry, Jesus took the disciples north to Caesarea Philippi. It was a remote district on the slopes of Mount Hermon. Jesus asked the disciples, "Who do people say the Son of Man is?" (Mt 16:13b). The group offered several opinions. Jesus pressed the question: "'But who do you say that I am?' Simon Peter answered, 'You are the Messiah, the Son of the living God'" (16:15-16). Peter got it first and he got it right. It was no accident he was a leader among the disciples. He had powerful insights and the courage to express them.

It is Thursday night. After Jesus gave his disciples the first Lord's Supper, he led them to the Mount of Olives. In a couple of hours, Judas would come with priests and soldiers. Jesus opened the conversation, "You will all become deserters because of me this night" (Mt 26:31). These words were almost a slap in the face. Jesus' indictment was that the disciples would run away, abandon him, and lose their nerve. Peter would not sit still for it. He retorts, "Though all become deserters because of you, I will never desert you" (Mt 26:33). Then Jesus told Peter, "this very night...you will deny me three times" (26:34). Peter was sure of himself. He said, "Even though I must die with you, I will not deny you" (26:35). Peter was not alone in his promise of faithfulness; "And so said all the disciples" (26:35b).

Peter was characteristically quick to speak, but as the events of the evening unfolded, Peter's words of loyalty turned false. Peter was cocky. He needed a little humility. Many people can identify with the need for humility. Where there is confidence to lead, there needs also be a touch of humility. An old preacher from North Carolina counseled young preachers with this advice "Don't tell them more than you know." A little humility is not only becoming, it represents us well. We are not infallible and events will prove it. We cannot predict how we will act in every situation. Peter couldn't and neither can we.

III. Humanity: We will all fail sometime.

Here is the setting of Peter's denial.

(1) Judas betrays Jesus with a kiss. There is a brief scuffle. Jesus is led away to the high priest's house. "All the disciples deserted him and fled" (Mt 26:56b).

(2) Peter fled, but followed closely behind. "But Peter was following him at a distance, as far as the courtyard of the high priest, and going inside, he sat with the guards in order to see how this would end" (Mt 26:58). Given the priests' hostility toward Jesus, Peter's following so closely was an act of courage. Other disciples stayed away.

(3) Three times Peter was challenged.

One
A servant-girl: "You also were with Jesus the Galilean."
Peter: "I do not know what you are talking about" (26:69).
The denial reads, "You have a case of mistaken identity."

Two
Another servant-girl: "This man was with Jesus of Nazareth."
Peter: Denial "with an oath," meaning he added, "So help me
God."

Three
Bystanders: "Certainly you are also one of them, for your accent
betrays you."
Peter: Denial, an oath and curses.

Eugene Boring notes that "'Curse,' used only here in the New
Testament...suggests that Peter cursed Jesus" (Boring, *The New
Interpreter's Bible*, Vol. 8, Nashville: Abingdon Press, 1995, 481).
Why did he do it? Peter did not offer excuses for himself, but I
will offer them for him.
• Peter was afraid. Out of fear, we do things we would not other-
wise do. The New Testament offers these words about fear, "Do
not be afraid," the resurrection greeting Jesus gave the disciples
(Mt 28:10). Or, "Perfect love casts out fear" (1 Jn 4:18). Again,
"God did not give us a spirit of cowardice..." (2 Tim 1:7a). The
Early Church had to face the power of Rome. It was frightening.
They had to manage their fears to fulfill Jesus' mission for them.
So do we. Out of fear, we still deny Jesus.
• Peter was tired. A few verses prior, Jesus is praying in the Garden
of Gethsemane (Mt 26:36-46). Peter could not stay awake. The
schedule, the tension, and the uncertainty wore him to a nub.
When Peter denied Jesus, his physical and mental conditions were
at their weakest. Peter's actions are not excused, but these
circumstances help explain them. We may not have control of our
physical condition all the time. When we care for a dying loved
one, we don't say, "I must not get over-extended." We give and we
give. But when stretched to the limit, we are vulnerable.
• Peter was despairing. He had invested everything in Jesus. His
fishing business was gone. Now Jesus was on trial and would
probably be killed. Peter had gambled everything on Jesus and
lost. Further, he loved Jesus. Watching the best person you've ever
known be framed and tried by a group of crooks does not make
for good judgment. He was confused.

• He was caught off-guard. Peter did not expect to be noticed. Peter was present because he loved Jesus. He never expected to be confronted. He wanted to fade into the woodwork.

Peter said he would never deny Jesus, but he did. Paul didn't live up to his words either (Rom 7:15). Neither do we.

IV. Hope: Peter got forgiveness and reassignment; we can, too.

Timing can be devastating. Peter had just denied Jesus for a third time and "At that moment the cock crowed. Then Peter remembered...And he went out and wept bitterly" (Mt 26:75b). I've know the sinking feeling of letting down a friend, but I've never had an experience like Peter's. The remorse, the self-loathing, the second-guessing must have haunted him. How could he face the other disciples after public boasting and craven cowardice? Peter had no easy way to go.

John's Gospel tells the end of the story. Resurrection came and Jesus appeared to the disciples several times. At the Sea of Galilee, Jesus shares breakfast with the disciples. He then turns to Peter as if to say, "Don't we have some unfinished business?" "Simon son of John, do you love me more than these?" (Jn 21:15). There had been three denials, so there were three questions: Do you love me? Peter was given the opportunity to say, "I love you" three times. It was almost as if Peter were saying "I love you" for every time he had said "I don't know you."

Jesus forgave Peter and gave him an assignment. After each "I love you" Jesus said "Feed my lambs....Tend my sheep....Feed my sheep" (Jn 21:15-17). Jesus predicted Peter would be bound for the gospel's sake. He would suffer. The past was over, forgotten. Peter was given a new page to write on and a fresh start. The book of Acts shows that Peter served magnificently.

Sometimes we make huge mistakes. We do a bad job of representing Jesus. This text affirms that God still can pick us up, clean us up and use us again. I find great hope in this text.

Notes

Notes

Other available titles from

NextSunday
Resources

1 Peter
Keep Hope Alive

This study of First Peter focuses on keeping hope alive in the face of pressures and circumstances that could possibly extinguish it completely, or worse, turn authentic faith into a pale replica of the real thing.

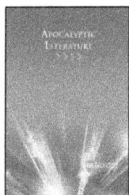

Apocalyptic Literature

This study examines five apocalyptic texts in the Bible—from Zechariah, Daniel, Matthew, and Revelation. With each new year bringing a new prediction of impending doom, it is always a perfect time to get the story straight. Apocalyptic literature does not address the future. It addresses our present.

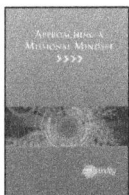

Approaching a Missional Mindset

The World isn't the same as it once was. We must be the church in a new place, in unimagined ways, and with a wider range of people. Engage your small group with the radical and refreshing challenge of developing a "missional lifestyle."

Baptist Freedom
Celebrating Our Baptist Heritage

What makes a Baptist a Baptist? Of course, the ultimate answer is simple: membership in a local Baptist church. But there are all kinds of Baptist churches! What are the spiritual and theological marks of a Baptist? What is the shape and the feel of Baptist Christianity?

Challenges of the Christian Life

The way of the cross is difficult, and taking Jesus seriously means looking honestly at how we fall short of God's best hopes for us and seeing how much we need God's grace. For all of us there are times when we need to remember that Christ is our saving grace and recommit ourselves to the journey of faith, rediscovering, again and again, the life-giving purpose described in the book of Ephesians.

Christ Is Born!

Even in the midst of difficult circumstances, Advent is a time when we can find hope. Much like today, people in the 1st century church faced struggles. Examining the Gospel of Matthew, lessons covered are "Waiting for Christ," "Preparing for Christ," "Expecting Christ," "Announcing Christ," and "The Arrival of Christ."

Christmas in Mark

In the early chapters of Mark, we will encounter a Christmas story. This story, however, will not be quite like the one told by other Gospel writers, but it will resonate with the reality of your life. Mark doesn't deny the beauty or reality of the nativity; however, he seems to believe that Christmas begins—the gospel begins—when Christ intrudes upon the hard realities of life.

Christians and Hunger

These sessions challenge us to apply gospel lenses and holy imagination to what literally gives us energy to live: food. With God's grace, we have the opportunity to imagine communities where tables are large and all are fed.

The Church on a Mission

What does it mean to be a church on a mission? The lesson of Acts 1:8 is that we must simultaneously carry out Christ's mandate at home, in our region, in places that have been our blind spots, and around the world.

Colossians
Living the Faith Faithfully

Paul's letter to the Colossians begins with a high-minded philosophical defense of the faith, but concludes with a collection of extremely practical advice for living by faith. This study addresses the questions many Christians face today, helping them apply Paul's practical advice in their own lives.

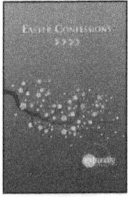

Easter Confessions

Easter confession is often found on many different lips in the Gospel of John. When we listen carefully, those ancient confessions still echo into this new millennium.

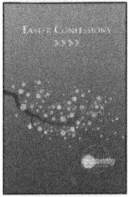

Embracing the Word of God

We live during a time of transition in Christian history. Basic assumptions about the truth of the Christian faith are being questioned, not only by nonbelievers, but by Christians themselves. First John offers a starting point for understanding of what it means to "be" Christian.

Esther: A Woman of Discretion and Valor

The book of Esther is not a record of historical facts as such. Rather, it is a magnificent narrative that refuses to interpret life as being driven by coincidence or happenstance. In the otherwise unknown characters of Esther, Haman, and Mordecai, we trace the movement of the divine hand as God collaborates with God's risk-taking people to rescue them from the hand of their enemies.

Facing Life's Challenges

This study explores four significant challenges common to most persons of faith: the challenge of new light, the challenge of time's limit, the challenge of living with mystery, and the challenge of authentic spirituality. Although these issues are neither simple nor easy to ponder, this study effectively leads us in confronting these challenges.

Galatians
Freedom in Christ

Paul wrote with fiery passion, as you will notice from the opening paragraphs of this letter to the Galatians. But his language reveals that he was writing about a crucially important issue—the very nature of salvation in Christ.

How Does the Church Decide?

An array of decisions draw energy and time from church members. These decisions may be theological, such as mode of baptism, aesthetic, such as the color of the sanctuary carpet, or functional, such as the selection of a new minister. This study will consider how the church has made its decisions in the past to help guide our decisions today.

A Holy and Surprising Birth

Christmas begins here—discover these five love stories and renew your appreciation of God's laborious effort to birth our salvation.

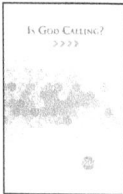

Is God Calling?

Witness the varying forms of God's call, the variety of people called, and the variety of responses. Perhaps God's call to you will become clearer.

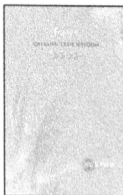

James
Gaining True Wisdom

If we'll be honest with God and ourselves as we study what James says, we can make great strides toward wisdom and a living faith.

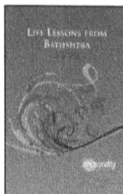

Life Lessons from Bathsheba

Who was Bathsheba? She was a complex figure who developed from the silent object of David's lust into a powerful, vocal, and influential queen mother.

Life Lessons from David

In the Bible, we catch David in the various stages of the human journey: childhood, adolescence, adulthood, and senior adulthood. From the biblical treatment of the stages of David's life, we can land some insights to assist us in better understanding the human journey.

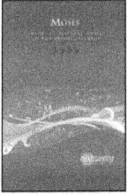

Moses
From the Burning Bush to the Promised Land

We would do well to trace the life of Moses so we might discover how his life changed, both personally and as Israel's leader, as he learned what it meant to love God with all his heart, soul, and strength.

Old Testament Promises to God

Some individuals may feel that our promises couldn't possibly mean anything to God. Perhaps the real question is this: under what circumstances should or do we make such promises? The Old Testament contains several examples of people making promises to God, using the unique form of a biblical "vow."

The Prayer Life of Jesus

The study of Jesus' prayer life can deepen our own prayer practices. These five sessions examine the importance of prayer at various stages of Jesus' life and ministry. He made no important decisions without consulting God.

Proverbs for Living

Long ago, a collection of wise teachers committed themselves to the ways of God and collect this wisdom into what we know as the book of Proverbs. These four lessons explore the simple truth of Proverbs: There is a good life to be had—a life lived in faithfulness to God.

Seeking Holiness in the Sermon on the Mount

The Sermon on the Mount has long been recognized as the pinnacle of Jesus' teaching. But with this importance in mind, it's easy to think of Jesus' teachings as lofty and idealistic, offering little guidance for everyday life. Perhaps Jesus' sermon allows us to see beyond ourselves, beyond our own failures and shortcomings—revealing God's intention for our lives.

Spiritual Disciplines
Obligation or Opportunity?

The spiritual disciplines help deepen a believer's faith and increases his or her intimacy with Christ. In this study, we take a deeper look at some of the disciplines and consider their practice as a response to God's love.

Stewardship
A Way of Living

Great News! Stewardship is not about money! At least not *just* about money. Certainly, stewardship relates to money, and, yes, we need to tithe. However, stewardship branches out into multiple areas of life. Properly practiced, this act of service can lead to peace and purpose in living.

The Ten Commandments

When the Ten Commandments are in the news, it is usually because a judge or teacher has hung them up on the walls. The Ten Commandments do not need to be posted or even preached nearly so much as they need to be practiced and viewed as life-giving, joyful affirmations of a better way of life.

www.ingramcontent.com/pod-product-compliance
Lightning Source LLC
Chambersburg PA
CBHW060659030426
42337CB00017B/2695